DECLUTTER YOUR MIND

SIMPLIFY YOUR THOUGHT PROCESS, ...NESS, AND TAKE CONTRO...

By K. C...

© Copyright 2018 By K. Connors - All Rights Reserved.

Copyright © 2018 *Declutter Your Mind.* All rights reserved. No part of this publication may be reproduced, distributed, or transmitted in any form or by any means, including photocopying, recording, or other electronic or mechanical methods, without the prior written permission of the publisher, except in the case of brief quotations embodied in critical reviews and certain other noncommercial uses permitted by copyright law. This also includes conveying via e-mail without permission in writing from the publisher. All information within this book is of relevant content and written solely for motivation and direction. No financial guarantees. All information is considered valid and factual to the writer's knowledge. The author is not associated or affiliated with any company or brand mentioned in the book, therefore does not purposefully advertise nor receives payment for doing so.

Table of Contents

INTRODUCTION 4
CHAPTER ONE 7
DECLUTTER YOUR MIND 7
CHAPTER TWO 15
STRATEGIES ON HOW TO DECLUTTER YOUR LIFE 15
CHAPTER THREE 19
TAKE CONTROL OF YOUR LIFE 19
CHAPTER FOUR 26
DON'T PROCRASTINATE - DO IT NOW 26
CHAPTER FIVE 31
PURSUING HAPPINESS 31
CHAPTER SIX 39
SIMPLIFY YOUR LIFESTYLE 39
CHAPTER SEVEN 44
DECLUTTER YOUR MIND BY DECLUTTERING YOUR HOUSE 44
CONCLUSION 46

INTRODUCTION

Many people will take certain rooms in the house and try to declutter and organize them. This makes sense because our houses can get out of order and this can cause a problem. If it makes sense to do this with your items in your home and closets, it also makes sense to do this with your mind.

The first thing that you need to do is to get your mind organized. For some, this can be done by simply thinking. For most people, this is done by writing down the things that you need to do. Get everything out of your mind onto paper which will help your mind feel better.

Try to start working on your to-do lists that you create. This will help you not have to constantly thinking about what you need to do and so you won't have to worry about what it is that you have to get done. Sometimes by getting things done, it helps.

You might just need to get some sleep if your mind feels overwhelmed or worried. Getting sleep will help your mind reorganize itself the way that it needs to be done.

Decide on what is important to you and start to focus on that. At times knowing that your mind is focused on something that matters can help.

Start the habit of journaling. This is a process where you can always be writing down what is on your mind. This helps you to have an outlet as well as something that allows you to reflect on things later on. Learn how to really relax. Find things that you can do that will help you settle down. Many times, this alone will take away the worry and let your mind feel much better.

Here are six ways to get you thinking about yourself, turning within, and decluttering the one thing that will truly set you free.

1. Don't think what is; think what you want to be. Focus on your goals, your dreams and your passions. There will always be a disconnect between how things are, and how you would like them to be.

Point your thoughts towards the latter and you will find that the distance between the two will become less apparent.

2. Let go of the past. Don't forget it, but let it go. What is past is prologue.

3. Simplify your thought process. The formula is simple. Keep positive thoughts in, and negative thoughts out.

4. Do not dwell on the things that you cannot control. This requires incredible discipline and is the hardest of all to accomplish. But you must try. If you are involved with something that is out of your control, something that you cannot immediately do something about, then get it out of your mind. Put it aside for a while, and the time will come when you can change it.

5. Discover your inner Self, and leave it at that. Sometimes it's OK to just focus on you for a while. Think about what moves you, what inspires you. What makes you most comfortable, creative, and productive? Focus on these things. Meditate extensively on them. You can start small by just dedicating ten minutes a day to really put your mind towards the things you want.

6. Don't be afraid to be alone. Solace can be extremely rewarding. Go to a movie by yourself. Treat yourself to a solo dinner. Spend significant time in solitude. When you do, your mind will wander, and you will begin to understand how your thought process really works. Having such an understanding is impossible if you are constantly surrounded by other people.

In order to truly be free, to be truly more productive, less stressed, to think clearly, and live simply and creatively, we must be willing to go that extra mile. Try to look at things in a different way. We must be willing to look inward, examine our own Self, and take the necessary steps to declutter our minds. Without doing this, all of the other measures you take can inevitably become temporary and finding real peace can be elusive.

CHAPTER ONE
DECLUTTER YOUR MIND

Just as people process and gather new information differently, each and every one of us has developed throughout our lives ways to organize our environment and move through our spaces. Nevertheless, the fact remains. We live buried in a multitude of "stuff". I believe that as long as our physical environment is in a constant state of clutter, our potential to generate successful ideas, find inspiration, and harness the motivation to put action plans in place would be severed.

To unclutter must be seen of as an exercise to look for ideas among all the stuff that is taking extra space in our lives, and therefore in our minds. Once space has been cleared out, you may have a closer look into what you have and determine its true purpose and worth. You may retain only the critical pieces that you need and assess the ways in which they may work better for you.

Just as you don't need a hundred dried out pens inside your drawer but just one pen that works great and writes smoothly, you do not need to keep your mind cluttered with negative or self-defeating thoughts, thoughts about projects that failed or did not get off the ground or simply thoughts about daily life activities, worries and stress that come when we fail to move on from unfinished projects or when we lack a true system to keep ourselves, our space, our lives and our ideas organized.

The connection between what our physical spaces look like and what it makes us feel cannot be denied. Moreover, these emotions may greatly affect not only the ways that we move through these spaces but what we do when we are in them. Put another way, if we don't feel comfortable in a room, if the room itself is in a disheveled state, has an unpleasant smell, or simply lacks the resources that we need to accomplish our purpose, then we'll end up doing nothing, or waste the most valuable thing we have, time, instead of making something happen.

I encourage you to invest your time wisely, and first tackle the clutter in your environment.

Then follow suit and re-organized your ideas. Creating a plan of action to declutter your physical space will work as a perfect exercise, later to be applied to your ideas. The foundations for your future success need to be built on well-prepared ground.

DECLUTTER YOUR LIFE FROM THE INSIDE OUT

Benefits of a decluttered mind:

The best place to begin to declutter your life is from the inside. Many people overlook the benefits that a healthy mind can offer. The mind can become bogged down with emotional baggage and seriously impact a person's ability to function. Decision-making can become a challenge and coping with problems may feel nearly impossible when you do not have a clear mental state. Therefore, it is important to learn how to free your mind of unnecessary clutter.

Since everyone is different, there is no one-size-fits-all method to clear your mind of clutter. However, the following are some common techniques that can begin you on your journey to decluttering your life by first decluttering your mind!

ALL IN GOOD TIME: SCHEDULES

Alleviate some of your mental stress by creating a schedule. When you have all tasks organized and planned out, with free time added in between, a significant amount of tension will be lifted. You will live more efficiently and suffer from fewer overwhelming moments. You cannot plan for everything and schedules must be altered from time to time. However, having a solid schedule for the things you know you must do, prioritized by importance, can make a huge difference in your mental stress. Plus, this is a great way of guaranteeing you have time set aside to practice your mind-decluttering techniques.

MEDITATION FOR A CLEAR MIND

Meditation is a popular tool to help declutter your life and your mind. You do not have to meditate the old-fashioned way. Try this more modernized technique: begin with music that you enjoy. Some people benefit from uplifting tunes or classic songs while others may prefer something edgier. The genre is entirely up to you, and it does not have to be relaxation music. Next, find a private area that you can isolate yourself from others and distractions.

Begin by playing the music. It is helpful to have a playlist, or you can loop the same song if you prefer as long as you do not have to get up and restart the music when the song ends. The music is acting as a guide to help you begin to declutter your life. Get comfortable on a bed, couch, chair or the floor. If you choose to lie down, make sure you do not fall asleep! Listen to the music as it fills the area around you. Close your eyes and focus on it. Allow your body to completely relax. It is best to lie on your back or sit with your arms limp to promote complete relaxation. Pick out an underlying sound in the song and follow it.

Let your mind become engulfed in it as you trail the sound through the song. This allows your mind and body to focus on something else while relaxing and enjoying good music.

USE WORDS TO REMOVE TENSION

Written words are a powerful tool to declutter your mind. How you use them is up to you. Some people prefer to write in a journal. This can be completely private and no one else has to see it. If you are concerned about others finding your written thoughts, consider jotting them down on a paper and then throwing it away or destroying it after you are done.

Another good way to use written words is to write letters. This is often done when negative feelings arise towards another person in your life. Once the letter is written, store it somewhere or throw it away. The idea is to get your feelings out on the paper, rather than on the person. This can actually work another way as well. When you are feeling depressed or down, pen a positive letter to a friend. This will help remind you of the good things so you can stay focused.

You can even send the letter if you want to! It is important to remember that when you declutter your life, you must strive to remove negative feelings and stay focused on the good things.

Begin to declutter your life now, starting with your mind. You will feel better, work more effectively and suffer from fewer setbacks. Plus, when bad things happen, you will be better equipped to handle them when your mind is clear of clutter.

DECLUTTER YOUR MIND AND FREE YOURSELF

We are constantly rushing around and our 'to do' list gets longer and longer. It is like a running commentary in our heads. That long list of jobs is never-ending, the pressure is mounting and we begin to feel like our heads are going to explode because it is all too much sometimes.

When this happens, you really do need to stop and take a step back and think carefully about what you are doing and why you are doing it. There is a lot of talk out there now about decluttering our homes to make our lives simpler.

Of course, it is true that if you get rid of clutter you begin to feel more in control of your life. But what about your mind?

You see, how can we begin to sort our homes out if we have so much going on in our heads that is holding us back and slowing us down? It comes down to the same thing. It's all about clearing your head so you can spend more valuable time on more important things.

At times, the weeks go by and we have so very much on our minds that we can never really focus on anything. Then we feel like we have 'lost' time, and this time will never come back. So we need to take action and reclaim some of that precious time for us.

So, how do we go about decluttering our mind?

1. Write a diary

I know we don't all like to write or feel we have no time to write but if you do have lots of anxieties or worries then writing them down can help you put everything into some sort of perspective. It clears up space in your mind so you can then use it for more satisfying things.

Try to set aside some time each day to write a few bits down. It will help in the future when you look back at when you did certain things.

2. Make a list

Declutter your mind by writing things in a list rather than keeping everything stored in your head. This way you won't have to remember everything all of the time.

3. Let go of negative thinking

This is very easy to do and it is a bad habit! It is draining. Not just for you but for everyone around you. Some events in your life can cause you to think negatively and it can take a lot of time and hard work to change your outlook.

It is you and you alone who is in charge of what goes through your mind. However, we still allow ourselves at times to become so engrossed in negative thoughts. You need to try very hard to let go of these negative thoughts whenever possible as it will relieve your mind of too much stress.

4. Just say 'no'

If you already have a lot going on then don't be tempted to add to it. Some of us just can't say 'no'. If someone asks something of you, just ask yourself if you can really take this on now. Sayings 'yes' all the time does become a habit and then you are stuck with doing it so start to train yourself to say 'no'.

5. Get on with it

Did you know that it is amazing how quickly you can do something once you finally commit to doing it? Believe me, thinking about doing something often uses up much more energy than actually doing it!

6. Avoid interruptions

At times, we feel like we are getting nowhere because we are constantly being interrupted. We all have cell phones these days so we are accessible 24 hours a day! Why? What on earth did we do before they came along? Our mind will overload in no time at all so try very hard to avoid where possible.

These are the main tips that we can try to use daily. Every little bit helps. Remember also to take breaks now and then. We all deserve a break. No one is going to give us a medal for working ourselves to the ground. Taking even a few minutes 'time out' from a task will help you to clear your thoughts and then you can come back more refreshed and ready.

By following simple tips like these, your head will no longer be full of clutter and too much information. By writing things down and taking action as soon as you can, you can declutter your mind and then you will have more opportunity to think about much more productive and enjoyable things.

There are four major areas of our lives that clutter tends to accumulate in. Let's address each of these areas individually.

1. Physical environment

Your physical environment consists of your home, office, and automobile.

Decluttering your environments includes tossing out the junk and organizing what you wish to keep. When you walk into your space, are you nurtured by it? Is it clean and decorated in a way that brings you peace and happiness? Decluttering your environment means that everything in it is in good working order. Right now, my vehicle needs several repairs and it affects me. My air conditioner doesn't work. The driver side's window doesn't open, the electric locks make a loud grinding noise, and the fuel injector pump is going out. Does my car run and get me around? It does, but it's annoying to have these loose ends not taken care of. I don't enjoy driving my car. How are your environments? Do they enable you to live healthily and happily?

2. Health and emotional balance

Your physical and emotional health is all about you. Decluttering yourself physically and emotionally means you are taking the steps to eat right, exercise regularly and take care of your mind and body. You are addressing any health concerns and keeping up with regular checks ups with your doctor. Decluttering forces you to address stress in your life. Do whatever it take to live a peaceful existence. Maintaining emotional balance includes managing your thought and emotional life - doing your best to keep your mind positive. It means that you are intellectually stimulating your brain, fostering creativity, and avoiding the things that are damaging to your mental state, like overworking or watching too much TV. When you've decluttered yourself, you look and feel good.

3. Money

Decluttering in the area of money requires us to maintain healthy financial habits. What is a healthy money manager? A healthy money manager has addressed all of her emotional issues with money. He/She is comfortable handling money, and uses her money wisely.

Decluttering requires you to address overspending or living in the dark when it comes to your financial picture. Having healthy financial habits means that you are saving money for both short term and long term needs. You have a will that addresses all of your assets, including your children. People in a healthy financial state understand the value of giving and not holding on to too tightly to money. Bills are paid on time, and debt is non-existent, with the exception of a mortgage. A healthy money manager is educated in wise investments or has a reliable and trusted financial advisor. Money is a tool that is necessary for you to live life in the way that is important to you.

3. Relationships

Relationships in your life include your family, friends, co-workers, and boss. Decluttering in the area of relationships means you are addressing any relationship problems and that you generally get along well with the people in your life. You have removed the relationships from your life that regularly drag you down or damage you. Keeping healthy relationships requires us to keep in touch with people in person, over the phone or email.

To declutter your relationships, you need to forgive everyone who has hurt you and put full closure to the relationships that are no longer in your life. Doing your part to maintain healthy relationships requires you to speak truthfully, avoid gossiping, and steer clear of criticizing and judging others. When we've decluttered our relationships, they provide the love and support that we need on this journey through life.

Take an honest look at your life. In what areas could you use a little decluttering? What needs to change to help you live your best life and be your best self?

CHAPTER TWO
STRATEGIES ON HOW TO DECLUTTER YOUR LIFE

Are you one of those people that live a life filled with clutter? Have you ever wanted to declutter your life but did not know where to start? It is a proven fact that to declutter your life you must first start by decluttering your mind. How many of you have read a magazine article or a news story that seemed to drift from topic to topic without any coherency? Some may point to such writing as an effective form of Avante garde material. However, most people will see that writing for what it truly is, which is undisciplined. Often, it is the result of a cluttered mind that lacks focus and is in need of decluttering.

Now, while you may notice such problems in others, can you notice such issues within yourself? Common signs of a cluttered mind include lack of concentration, forgetfulness, anger management issues, anxiety, and restlessness. Basically, the mind is not operating in the proper manner it should. This leads to the aforementioned behavioral problems.

That is why it is so helpful to take steps to reduce the psychic noise and to embrace the benefits of a decluttered mind.

Of course, this raises questions as to how to declutter your mind. The steps are not as tough as you might assume. Here are a few ways to take proper action.

1. Believe it or not, a lack of sleep can lead to a severely cluttered mind. Some may think they can perform effectively with little sleep. However, studies have proven that for most people, this is not the case. By going too long without the proper amount of rest, you undermine your ability to have coherent thoughts.

2. It seems like you cannot pass a convenience store aisle without buying numerous energy drinks. If you want to reap the benefits of a decluttered mind, stay away from these types of stimulants. Excess stimulant ingestion can lead to anxiety and racing thoughts, which can make a mind thoroughly cluttered. A

calm mind is generally not cluttered. Why ingest stimulants that undermine your ability to maintain a placid mind?

3. Exercise is a common way to declutter your mind. Some may find this a little hard to believe and assume that exercise only impacts the physical body. This is not the case, as a healthy body often begets a healthy mind. Performing exercises can reduce any anxiety you may be feeling that causes issues and a lack of clarity in your thinking.

4. Engaging in a little relaxing entertainment can also calm the mind. It can even allows the mind to operate more effectively. No, you do not want to waste hours watching television, listening to music, or reading magazine articles, but investing some time into leisurely pursuits that will prevent burnout and aid in reducing the clutter of the mind.

5. Increasing your critical analysis skills can also declutter the mind. This can be done in a number of ways. The process can range from something as esoteric as studying advanced mathematics to simply performing crossword puzzles. Really, anything that sharpens the mind will make it stronger and less cluttered. Among the many benefits of a decluttered mind is being mentally sharp and always on your game. That is why anything that strengthens the mind is well worth exploring.

6. Calming and relaxing activities such as meditation and yoga are popular because of their impact on the mind. Such activities have been developed through centuries of cultivation. That means they have long since refined the ability to calm one's mind and eliminate potential clutter. So, why not integrate such activities into your daily regimen?

Ultimately, the greatest of benefits of a decluttered mind is that you can live your life to the fullest without the psychological issues a mind that lacks calmness is known to embody. Rather than suffer in such a manner, it would be best to take the steps to calm the mind and enjoy the benefits such a perspective would deliver.

QUICK WAYS TO STAY FOCUSED AND DECLUTTER YOUR MIND

Everyday we are bombarded with things. Some of these things are important and some just aren't. Let's choose a better word; situations. However, the challenge comes when we put a higher level of importance on some situations that really aren't that important.

Such situations then become distractions away from those things/situations that we really ought to be focusing on. That's right. They take your mind on a path away from what is important to you without you realizing.

So here are 7 quick ways to stay focused and declutter your mind:

1. Prioritize

Take a few minutes be it 15 - 30 minutes every night before bed or even in the morning after waking to set out the tasks that you want to accomplish. Assign a level of priority to each and carry them out in the order of most important first down to the least important. If new tasks come up as you go through the day, then see where they fall into your other priorities for the day.

2. Stay calm

Yes, it may be hard to stay calm when things seem to be going crazy. But worrying does more harm than good. Think about it. How much have you gotten accomplished whilst your were worrying?

Chances are, not that much. So don't clutter your mind with situations that you have no control over, because you have no control over them.

3. Stay positive

Keeping a positive outlook on life does help with decluttering your mind. It actually links back to help you stay calm. You can stay positive and keep your mind free from clutter by reading what benefits you and not the latest gossip column. Keep positive people in your circle of friends and negative people at a distance.

4. Be grateful

When was the last time you actually acknowledged the things in your life that you have to be thankful for? Overall, being thankful for the good that has happened to you in your life goes a long way towards just helping you feel better and decluttering your mind. Why? Well, you don't spend time wanting this and that. Start being thankful and see how it goes.

5. Be real

Yes, being genuine is a great way to declutter your mind because you don't spend energy being anxious all the time worrying about how to impress people. Besides, you might be amazed at how much people might actually like and respect you for you.

6. Forgive and forget

This helps to keep you in a positive state. Itmight not be the easiest of things to do but at least you can begin to heal. Some say that keeping a grudge is like drinking poison and expecting the other person to die. It just doesn't work, so let go of the anger and pain.

7. Get it done

Take action now. Mike Litman has the phrase "You don't have to get it right, you just have to get it going". I think that says it all. Do something that gets you closer towards your goals and being able to tick off the items you plan for yourself to accomplish. Just taking action gets you so much closer towards decluttering your mind.

CHAPTER THREE
TAKE CONTROL OF YOUR LIFE

Each of us makes hundreds, if not thousands, of decisions every single day. Everything from when to get out of bed in the morning to when to go to bed at night requires a decision.

So it's easy to understand that our actions require decisions. But it is not quite so easy to understand that our feelings and emotions require decisions, too.

Many times, our emotions and feelings are simply reactions. But we can learn to direct our feelings and emotions, just as we do our actions, by taking the time to decide how we will feel and react to things.

Today, when you notice you are simply reacting to something rather than consciously choosing or deciding how you feel about it, stop and change your reaction if it isn't a reaction that will help you reach your goals.

For example, if you didn't manage to complete everything on your to-do list yesterday, and you feel depressed about it, stop and change that reaction or way of thinking.

Instead, celebrate all of the things that you did manage to accomplish. You'll probably be surprised at how good you suddenly start to feel!

Before you do anything else today, decide to have a wonderful day, no matter what you have planned. Even if a dental appointment is on your schedule, decide to make this a pleasant event.

Remember, it isn't so much what happens to us in life that matters. It's how we deal with what happens, and our attitude about it all that really matters.

Take charge of your life today and decide what you want to think, feel, and do.

WHAT DOES IT TAKE?

What does it take to take charge of your life? When does it make sense to make the kind of changes that taking charge of your life implies? When you want to take charge of your life, you will have questions that you need to answer.

1. Courage and confidence

It takes courage and confidence to take charge of your life. You might not feel an abundance in these areas right now if you're looking at taking charge of your life. Yet, you have been courageous and confident during previous times in your life. Life requires courage! Life demands confidence!

Courage enables you to consider what might be a better set of choices. Courage gives you the getup and go to pick yourself up and take action. Courage does not replace fear. Instead, courage allows you to go forward despite the fear that might be suggesting that it's too risky to move in the direction of your dreams.

Confidence allows you to use your talents and abilities in new ways. Confidence puts your skills to work in different circumstances. Confidence does not remove doubt. Rather, confidence allows you to do what you know how to do. Regardless of the doubt that you may be feeling.

This is in spite of reminders that today's circumstances are not precisely identical to how you've used your skills in the past.

2. Change

Change is inevitable. Life is filled with changes. Over the course of your lifetime, you'll live in an environment that presents many things to you, sometimes overwhelming you with the sense that your entire life is filled with change. As you face challenges and deal with change, it makes sense to adapt to the new situations that arise.

QUICK WAYS TO STAY FOCUSED AND DECLUTTER YOUR MIND

Everyday we are bombarded with things. Some of these things are important and some just aren't. Let's choose a better word; situations. However, the challenge comes when we put a higher level of importance on some situations that really aren't that important.

Such situations then become distractions away from those things/situations that we really ought to be focusing on. That's right. They take your mind on a path away from what is important to you without you realizing.

So here are 7 quick ways to stay focused and declutter your mind:

1. Prioritize

Take a few minutes be it 15 - 30 minutes every night before bed or even in the morning after waking to set out the tasks that you want to accomplish. Assign a level of priority to each and carry them out in the order of most important first down to the least important. If new tasks come up as you go through the day, then see where they fall into your other priorities for the day.

2. Stay calm

Yes, it may be hard to stay calm when things seem to be going crazy. But worrying does more harm than good. Think about it. How much have you gotten accomplished whilst your were worrying?

Chances are, not that much. So don't clutter your mind with situations that you have no control over, because you have no control over them.

3. Stay positive

Keeping a positive outlook on life does help with decluttering your mind. It actually links back to help you stay calm. You can stay positive and keep your mind free from clutter by reading what benefits you and not the latest gossip column. Keep positive people in your circle of friends and negative people at a distance.

4. Be grateful

When was the last time you actually acknowledged the things in your life that you have to be thankful for? Overall, being thankful for the good that has happened to you in your life goes a long way towards just helping you feel better and decluttering your mind. Why? Well, you don't spend time wanting this and that. Start being thankful and see how it goes.

5. Be real

Yes, being genuine is a great way to declutter your mind because you don't spend energy being anxious all the time worrying about how to impress people. Besides, you might be amazed at how much people might actually like and respect you for you.

6. Forgive and forget

This helps to keep you in a positive state. It might not be the easiest of things to do but at least you can begin to heal. Some say that keeping a grudge is like drinking poison and expecting the other person to die. It just doesn't work, so let go of the anger and pain.

7. Get it done

Take action now. Mike Litman has the phrase "You don't have to get it right, you just have to get it going". I think that says it all. Do something that gets you closer towards your goals and being able to tick off the items you plan for yourself to accomplish. Just taking action gets you so much closer towards decluttering your mind.

Taking charge of your life has to do with adjusting to the change as it occurs. Dramatic sudden change can leave your mind spinning. This is one time when taking charge of your life demands that you reach for all of the courage and confidence that you can muster.

3. Skills

You'll need to learn new skills. Times of change instill new skills. You can decide that you're willing to use your courage and confidence to gain the skills you need.

In fact, deciding is taking charge of your life because that is what makes it happen. I've found that when I reach deep for courage and confidence, I can decide to take action. I take charge of my life! I find that that leads to happiness.

TIPS ON HOW TO TAKE CHARGE OF YOUR LIFE NOW

If you want to live a successful life and achieve all the goals that you have set, this would be the right chapter for you. You are going to learn the 5 golden tips of how you can take charge of your life now. As long as you follow through these 5 guidelines below, you will have no problem making all your goals and dreams come true.

1. Find out what you want to accomplish in your life. Every successful person knows exactly what they want, and this is how they are able to focus all their energy to create amazing results in life. If you do not know where you want to go, you will never get going in the right direction. This is the main reason people are not accomplishing much in life.

2. Spend more time doing something productive that will bring you one step forward towards your goals. Knowing what you want is one thing, doing it is

another. Do you know that successful people spend most of their time doing something that will give them the results that they want in life? Ordinary people will spend time doing unnecessary stuff such as watching television, playing games, etc. Never let this happen to you.

3. Always practice the positive attitude of 'can do'. No matter whom you are and where you are from, you can and able to accomplish your goals and live your dreams if you want to. The most important key to making your dreams a reality is to fully believe that you can do it. If you do not have the right attitude, you will sabotage yourself and are not going to produce great results in life.

4. Adopt the habit of constant and never-ending improvement. Do you know that successful people have the habit of constantly learning? They read books, talk, research, train, and learn from all sorts of sources to improve themselves all the time. So start to read and learn about your industry so that you can become an expert in what you do.

5. Be prepared to sacrifice for the success that you want. Do you know that the moment you spend watching movie, some other people are working hard out there to achieve greater success? Great accomplishments will not come to you automatically. You must take action and be willing to sacrifice your leisure time to build the success that you want. No pain, no gain.

STEPS TO SUCCESS BY TAKING CHARGE OF YOUR LIFE

In this part, we'll go through the 4 steps that will help you "take off" in the right direction. Make no mistake - if you are completely serious about taking charge of your life, and finding the success you're looking for, the tips presented in our series will put you on the right path.

1. Set S.M.A.R.T. goals

Once you have acquired clarity of vision and purpose, the next step to achieving success is to specifically define S.M.A.R.T. goals. The acronym 'SMART' stands for Specific, Measurable, Achievable, Realistic, and Time-Sensitive. Identifying what you want and determining S.M.A.R.T. goals as benchmarks is another key to achieving success. If you don't have a clear roadmap of where you're going, you're likely to end up anywhere but your intended destination!

2. Defer

In addition to making your plan, you also need to develop a direction to your action plan. This will keep you motivated to keep going forward at all times. Although you may need some self-discipline to accomplish this, it is a vital aspect of any kind of achievement. Before beginning any new activity, examine it to see if it will help in moving you closer to the goals you have in mind. If it doesn't, you may need to put it aside for another time.

Deferring, delegating, or to deleting are the 3 D's taught by many personal and business coaches. If a certain activity can be put away for a later time, defer it. If that activity can be done by somebody else, delegate it. If it does not really need to be done at all, delete it. This kind of examination of each activity will help keep you focused on the things that are really important.

3. Decide on the course of action

One of the first steps in the process of successfully taking control of your life is to make the decision to move from where you are now to where you want to be, personally and professionally. All of us know that nothing happens until that first decision is made. Acknowledging your decision is a basic step, but it is often one many people tend to overlook. So, decide that you will move forward, put your decision in writing to keep it in focus, and then continue in a positive direction from there.

4. Take action

This final step is the catalyst to transforming your personal or professional life into whatever you want it to be. Absolutely nothing can be attained or achieved until action is taken. By putting your plan of action into motion, you will gain control over your own life and confidently headed down your road to success!

It's a wonderful feeling when you know you are becoming the successful "C.E.O. of Your Life" and that you are finally back in the driver's seat.

WAYS TO TAKE CHARGE OF YOUR LIFE AND YOUR SCHEDULE

How can you give your attitude and your life a boost of energy?

Do you wish you had a few more hours' everyday?

Do you waste too much time looking for things?

Do you feel overwhelmed by paper and stuff?

Do you often feel drained at the end of the day?

Are you constantly reacting to life?

Develop a power hour once a week to help you organize your time and your life so that you have more time for living!

These few simple suggestions will help you challenge the ways you spend your time and offer you constructive ways to help you gain control over your time This is an inspirational approach to time management.

These strategies will help you gain control over your time and provide additional hours in your day.

10 ways to help you create better time management, organization and prioritized living

1. Deal with email and mail overload
2. Handle interruptions
3. Sort, purge and organize your "stacks"
4. Get uncluttered

5. Overcome procrastination
6. Say no and set boundaries
7. Plan your week and your day
8. Create time for your priorities
9. Set short-term goals
10. Be more present in your life

Get in the habit of setting time limits for the tasks needing to be completed. Have a kitchen timer in your office and keep track of how much time you spend on personal calls, answering emails, and on individual projects.

CHAPTER FOUR
DON'T PROCRASTINATE - DO IT NOW

TIPS TO PREVENT OR MINIMIZE PROCRASTINATION

Procrastination! Don't you just love that word? We all do it or have done it in the past. Some people procrastinate all the time, some just sometimes. A few have recognized that they procrastinate, and with a desire to prevent or minimize it. They take measures to achieve what they want to do in the timeframes they want. When it comes to achieving success, procrastination is the most common problem to failure, because it is so easy to do.

WHAT IS PROCRASTINATION?

The definition of procrastination is, "To habitually put off doing something until a future time." I am guilty of procrastinating sometimes. But I have gotten a lot better because of my huge desire to achieve the kind of success I want in life. I will be sharing some of the tips that I learned to help me prevent or minimize procrastination.

Do you procrastinate on things? Why do you feel you do it? Do you want to minimize it?

"Old man procrastination stands within the shadow of every human being, waiting his opportunity to spoil one's chances of success." - Napoleon Hill

People procrastinate on many things, especially the ones that involve more effort or don't have any immediate gratification. Procrastination carries a high potential for undesired consequences in all areas of your life when it comes to success. It can lead to feelings of guilt and self-doubt, which in turn can lead to lost opportunities. Procrastination is a serious problem when it comes to success in your business and many other areas of your life.

SO WHY DO WE PROCRASTINATE?

Well, one reason is that it is so easy to do. A lot of us love to avoid pain or things that involve a lot of work or attention. In business, most people procrastinate, especially when prospecting. Many times, especially in the beginning, that phone feels like it weighs 20 pounds!

Another common reason is poor time management. When you hear people say, "I don't have enough time," they simply have bad time management. Everyone has the same 24 hours in a day. Why is it that some people get so much more done in that same 24 hours than others? Good time management. They are certain of their priorities, goals, and objectives. Get off the couch, turn off that TV, and get to work!

Here's another reason: perfection. The definition, "Demanding perfection in all things, especially his or her own work." I am guilty of this, and I know many people are. There are still times right now when I have a little "writer's block" when I am writing books. Not everything has to be perfect. In fact, you don't have to be perfect to become highly successful in anything, and especially your business/life. In sports, even the All-Star athletes are not perfect. In basketball, a 50% field goal percentage is great. In baseball, a .300 batting average (out 7 out of 10 times at the plate when batting) is paid millions of dollars a year! How about your business?

TIPS TO PREVENT OR MINIMIZE PROCRASTINATION

Here are some tips that I have learned and apply to help me to prevent or minimize procrastination. Apply these, and you will have less procrastination and be able to get more things done to help you towards your goals and success.

1. Personal development: This is key to getting your mind right and keeping it staying right. This will help you realize what you are doing and why you are doing it, and help to keep you motivated and tough enough to apply these tips to

preventing or minimizing procrastination. Read books, attend events, get on webinars and conference calls, etc. Invest in yourself!

2. Prioritize: Write down the things that you need to get done in the order of importance. Don't just think of it. Write it down! Put that list in a place where you will see it often. Make copies and put it in more areas, and even carry one with you if you are out.

3. Identify tasks you can avoid: Avoid time wasters during productive times, and put them off until the slow times, or later in the night. Those are things like checking email, or "playing around on. Facebook." I personally use Facebook as one of my top marketing methods, but I do what I need to do on there and stick to the time schedule I set for being on Facebook.

4. Be realistic: Don't set unrealistic expectations when it comes to completion dates and times. Give yourself enough time to realistically achieve what you are looking to complete.

5. Start small: Break down large tasks, and tackle one piece at a time. Tasks can seem overwhelming when looked at as one large one to complete. Break it down to smaller projects with specific goals. Your attention span will be much better when you do that. Don't bite off more than you can chew.

6. Minimize distraction: All of us have busy lives, and many responsibilities. Try to eliminate as much distraction as you can during your productive times. Put your phone to voicemail, turn off the TV and radio, close and lock your door, close your email program, etc. This will get you more focused, and you will get more done faster and more efficiently.

7. Don't wait: Of course, the time will never be "just right." Remember, don't worry about perfection. Just start and be human.

8. Take some time off: Don't overwork yourself. Take a day off with no work. On that day, don't even think of work. Just enjoy what you are doing and be free. Of course, if you are in network marketing, and are already doing pretty good, you will have income coming in on that day whether you are personally working

or not. So that will make it even easier to just be free and just have fun during that whole day, or week, or month, etc:)

9. Reward yourself: After you accomplish your goals, reward yourself a little. Motivation requires motive. Choose a reward for completing a task, and ensure yourself a good reward for completing it. Go out to a movie, a nice dinner, or other pleasures that you love. You will feel refreshed and focused!

10. Just do it: Yes, just do it! Remember, don't be a perfectionist. Don't worry about the end result in the beginning. Just get started. Once you start, things will start to get easier and easier.

Apply these tips to your business and your personal life to prevent or minimize procrastination, and you will achieve more success. One of the number one attributes of every top earner in every network marketing company is that they don't procrastinate most of the time. When it comes to prospecting time, they get it done. They prioritize their time and tasks. You can do the same as well.

STOP PROCRASTINATING AND IMPLEMENT IMMEDIATELY

Just do it! Pick one small step and work on until it is finished. Move on to the next.

Set a realistic period of time to complete each step. Set your computer or smartphone to chime halfway through the allotted time. Step back and assess what you're doing, then adjust as necessary.

Do it badly if necessary. A lot of procrastinators are also perfectionists. Remember; you can always go back and tweak it later.

Let me remind you that every one of us is capable of taking small steps and by setting a time limit it makes it easier to meet your specific goal. I think this is true because it forces you to keep your focus. Taking small steps also has the added benefit of causing a snowball effect. With each step, you complete you gain confidence and become more motivated to move on to the next step. Before you know it, one section, and then another, is done until the task is finished.

Taking small steps - that is the key that will help you to stop procrastinating, now the only thing left to do is give yourself a pat on the back, choose a new task and repeat the process.

CHAPTER FIVE
PURSUING HAPPINESS

Everyone in this world is in constant pursuit of happiness. Yet, the ones who find it are the ones who realize they already have it. It is a commonly accepted fact that people smile when they are in a good mood. Happiness is not all about smiling. There are several smile specialists out there like orthodontists who can fix any problem with a person's smile. Yet, that does not guarantee happiness. People look great when they are smiling but being content is something that makes everything look much better. There are not any Cosmetic dentists who can make a person happy at any cost. It is up to you to make your life more satisfied.

How can one make his or her life more fulfilling? Is there a secret to happiness? The answer is yes, there is not just one but seven secrets of how to end the eternal pursuit of happiness. These are all small little changes a person can bring to his or her life in order to be more satisfied and content with whatever life is offering.

1. All the secrets for being happy revolve around one main concept: optimism. In the first place, a person should be optimistic about one's own self. Having a respectable level of self-respect and loving yourself for the person you are; is the key to finding happiness. If there is something that you think is not worth being happy about, then try to change it.

2. Avoiding grudges is the second stepping stone towards the temple of happiness and bliss. Forget people's mistakes, and try to focus on their positive points instead. Sooner or later, you will realize that life is not a movie and no one intends to be the evil villain deliberately.

3. Always look at the brighter side of life. Do not whine over things you wanted and could not get. Be cheerful about the things that you are blessed with without even asking. Look around and you will surely find people deprived of what you have got.

4. Try to make people happy. In general, people do not need expensive gifts and surprises to be pleased. A warm greeting or a friendly smile is enough to make someone's day. And getting them back will surely make yours as well.

Connect with everyone around you such as friends, family and even strangers. Public admiration is definitely a happiness booster.

5. Be honest. In every aspect of life, try to stay away from fears and guilt. Avoid cheating, lying, and dishonesty. This rule applies to family, love and even the workplace. Enjoy your work and try not to go to bed with any unfinished business at hand.

6. If you want to do anything or change anything. Just do it. Even if you are not sure of the results, just go with your gut rather than staying confused.

7. Choose to be more optimistic. It is all about how you choose to act and react. There are always two kinds of responses and reactions to a situation: the calm and happier one and the angry and frustrated one. At any given time and situation, it is you who can choose to be happy or not.

TIPS TO PURSUE HAPPINESS

In my opinion, happiness is a simple mind, a plain attitude; however, it's also not easy to catch sometimes. Only if we have known how to pursue happiness, can we live with happiness together! I'm sincere in sharing the tips to pursue happiness with you here.

1. Be optimistic

To be optimistic is the most important factor in the pursuit of a happy lifestyle. It's inevitable to meet various kinds of troubles when we are growing. Different minds can bring distinct effects. For example, if you are optimistic and positive enough, you can be a promising winner even you just had a failure. In reverse, you will be a loser once again if you can deal with the present failure optimistically.

2. Be strong

The stronger you are able to be, the more easily you will attain happiness. "Strength" is meant to build a stronger body and an emphasis on the strength of your capability.

There is no doubt that you are unlikely to be happy if you are ill or weak. Similarly, you are very likely to feel diffident if you are not strong enough to show your ability in your work or study. I believe in strength having a dispensable role in the pursuit of happiness.

3. Be friendly

A happy life can never exist without a friendly mind, just as a person can never be happy if he/she has no friends. Here, to be friendly doesn't narrowly mean to be kind to just your friends. Deeply, it means to be kind to all the people around you, especially those who are in the need of help. Giving a hand to the pitiful guys, and you will experience the happiness of making a contribution to others.

Happiness is not a destination. Compared with the result, the process to get a happy life, instead, is much more significant!

PURSUING HAPPINESS - WHAT TO AVOID?

Everyone wants to be happy, but their happiness must not cause other people's suffering, otherwise it is a selfish happiness that is not real.

As a matter of fact, the contradictions that one finds when searching for happiness are the most important stages of this journey because people tend to neglect other people's happiness when thinking about their own. This indifference is responsible for many conflicts that cause pain and even tragedies, especially concerning relationships with married people.

At this point, we can verify how indispensable moral principles are since they are the only guides we have when we face the numerous contradictions that appear in our way. Respect for other people's lives, their companions, and their belongings is the only way the human being must protect and guarantee one's psychic health. Without psychic health and peace, real happiness cannot exist.

If one person's happiness means someone else's pain, this happiness is threatened all of the time. It is unfair, and it will cause remorse.

If it doesn't cause remorse, things are not better but worse, because one must be sensitive and empathize with other people's pain in order to be balanced and not cause conflicts and despair in their environment.

A fair happiness is based on what everyone feels. So, in cases when conflicts emerge from what makes someone happy, the conflicts must be avoided and the person has to understand that their desires are not noble as they are not for the well being of everyone involved.

If a person thinks about this matter with a selfish intent, they will conclude that they do not care about how other people feel but only about how they feel. However, happiness based on what is bad for someone else is completely false and condemned to disappear beneath all the problems that will arise from such a contradiction.

If they think that they can simply ignore other people's suffering and be indifferent to the unjust way they acted against them, their happiness is cold and cruel and is something that certainly won't last for long.

Real happiness comes only when everyone respects everybody's feelings.

The right person for everyone exists and can be found, but only if they are not misled by their selfish and ephemeral desires which may not be real but only an illusion provoked by the wild and evil part of their conscience that is always trying to induce craziness to the human side of their conscience.

One must be very careful when pursuing one's desires because one may be only following the wild conscience's plan, which will imprison one in the labyrinth of craziness and fill his life with despair, instead of providing him with the promised happiness.

Only when we are morally correct can we have peace of mind and hope to build a really happy life, far from the dangers of craziness. But we never know what to do when facing life's obscure challenges.

That's why we always need the wise orientation from the unconscious that produces our dreams, which can guide us in the dangerous path that is always threatened by many temptations, showing us where we can find real happiness and keep it for life.

HAPPINESS HABITS

Exactly how do we pursue happiness? We know happiness is far more than just money, fame or power. There are lots of people who have all three who are not especially happy. What are the secrets to living a happy and successful life? Are there reliable road maps to the state of happiness?

If you want to live a happy life, study happy people. Observe what they do, understand why it works so well and then adopts their behaviors and beliefs. We can choose to pursue and cultivate habits and skills we know will lead to happy and successful lives.

Cultivate a sense of fun and share it with everyone you meet. Habitually happy people truly try to have a good time all of the time. Critics cry;

"Don't be silly, you can't expect to have a good time all of the time!" Habitually Happy people reply, "I can!" Or, "with an attitude like that, you will never be really Up or happy!"

Exercise your freedom to choose happiness. Decide who you want to be, what sort of person you want to become. Define yourself as a happy and successful person. Let that goal become a sort of role that is real and authentic for you. Try to be your best successful self all of the time. If we don't consciously decide what sort of person we want to be, then our environment and experiences define our identity and destiny for us.

Rebel against people or situations that try to drag your spirits down. Don't hand control of your thoughts, actions, feelings, and well-being over to annoying people or outside circumstances that can rob your happiness. Cultivate an indomitably strong, independent and positive good spirit.

Choose emotional independence. Decide how you want to think and feel. There's no rule that says just because something bad happens, you have to feel sad.

Remember, you must be at your best to do your best. Choose actions and attitudes that help you to succeed and be happy.

Make goodness a guiding goal. We are amazed how truly happy genuinely good people are. "Goodness for goodness sake," one said. Habitually happy people are extraordinarily kind, caring and compassionate. The Dutch proverb "Happy people are never wicked" was proven by our research.

Give freely and without strings attached. Habitually happy people are genuinely altruistic; they do good for the joy of doing good. They give without strings attached, they do not give just in order to get. Goodness is its own reward. They rarely pass up an opportunity to be kind when it costs or risks them little.

Don't be a people pleaser. Enjoy sharing joy and making other people happy, but don't depend on other people's approval to be happy yourself. Feel good by knowing and appreciating your achievements and all the things you do well.

Take care of yourself and value yourself. Habitually happy people value their time, their talents and their resources. They continually seek to develop themselves, strengthen their skills and gain a greater understanding of the world and the people around them. They value other people's time and resources as much as they value their own.

Be adventuresome. Habitually happy people continually explore, try new things and do new things to stay fresh and to continually experience difference and change. It helps them grow and maintain their enthusiasm and positive spirits.

One commented, "I get bored with the same old stuff, I want each day to be new, different, something special." They try to make each day special.

Don't beat yourself up. Habitually happy people move from problems to solutions quickly. They know that time spent dwelling on problems tends to reinforce the mistakes they want to avoid. They don't condemn themselves for errors. They channel their angst over mistakes toward finding solutions or rectifying problems. They do not intentionally hurt themselves.

Avoid the fault finding feel goods - Criticism, blame, ridicule, bigotry, all falsely elevate our sense of power and self-worth by finding fault with something else. These feel goods are fed by a negative focus. You cannot be truly happy by continually finding fault, focusing on what's wrong, judging or criticizing. Habitually happy people don't complain and they avoid people who do.

Have high integrity and live according to your values. When you live by the highest and best values you can feel confident that, even if you stumble, you have done your best. Few things are worse than compromising your integrity and then failing too. Habitually happy people cherish good values and they live by them. They know happiness only comes with a clear conscience.

Love is an active verb. Love is an action; it is something we decide to do. It is an emotion we can choose to feel and to project and share with others. Love can be expressed in everything we do. It's not just something that happens to us. Love propels happiness. The more we love, the happier we become.

Don't be a snob. Value everyone. Happy people don't have to feel better than others in order to feel good about themselves. They try to find something of interest and value in everyone they meet. They try to touch each person they meet with a smile and a bright, positive spirit.

Continually celebrate success. Habitually happy people continually celebrate success, their own and other people's successes. This fuels everyone's positive energy, confidence, and desire to do well and propels people to achieve more. Celebrating success provides positive role models.

CHAPTER SIX
SIMPLIFY YOUR LIFESTYLE

When you think about simplifying your life, what comes to mind? Getting rid of things you really don't need? Doing less, spending less, downsizing, and consolidating? All of these are noteworthy ways to simplify, but they can have a negative undertone if it feels like you have to give something up. Without realizing it, this could be your inner vibration, so let's look at these endeavors from a positive place.

When we rid ourselves of what we no longer need, we actually open up space for new to enter, not to mention the blessing that we bestow on another as they receive those items. Perhaps it's time for you to step into your real work or give to it more fully rather than so much emphasis and time on trivialities and trying so hard to please others. Could you benefit by saving more and thus be prepared for uncertain times, such as we are experiencing now, rather than stressing over making ends meet or keeping in step with the image you've created?

What about time to "just be", when you quietly tune into your higher self and connect with your source instead of being busy? So rarely do any of us take the time to tap into our inner resources and hear what our spirit is telling us.

Changing your focus to the positive perception is freeing and raises your vibration to a higher level. Isn't that what you really want? Isn't that the cry being echoed across our great nation - a cry for freedom? Simplicity frees you from the self-imposed "have tos", "musts", "shoulds", rules and restrictions; it's a place where you are able to use your inborn power of choice. Everything in our life is created by our thoughts and choices, so it's up to each of us to be conscious of those thoughts and what we are creating. If we don't like what we are experiencing, then we have to change our thoughts which will then change and our behavior.

The universe is telling us to wake up and the planetary alignments of recent months have perpetuated a major shift that will continue for months to come.

We are being told to let go of what isn't working and to create a new paradigm. People like to feel secure and comfortable, so letting go usually doesn't feel too good.

Yet, letting go of things - relationships, old patterns and old beliefs - is the only way to open up a space for something new to enter your life. This is what is happening now. Time to let go.

So what isn't working for you right now? Are you experiencing a relationship that doesn't raise you up and you need to let go of it, but you're scared to do it? Is it time to step into your purpose for being here in this lifetime, but again, you're afraid of taking that step? Do you fear the void in your life if you let go of something you're used to having? Indecision will stop your growth and keep you from the wonderful new life you can now experience!

In the midst of all our chaos shines a bright light that is leading us to a better life and world, one that we now have the opportunity to create. What a glorious adventure! Along with others, I feel we are being guided into a more simplistic, pure life, back to the basics, where our roots are, as we rebuild a strong foundation based on truth and freedom. Simplifying your life is an opportunity to create an extraordinary life!

WAYS TO SIMPLIFY YOUR LIFESTYLE

What would a simpler life look like for you? Fewer obligations? Fewer possessions? Fewer bills? As our world shifts into a time of refreshing, purging and simplifying, we will find that our lifestyles shift with it. Below are my top 10 ways to simplify your lifestyle (in no particular order). You can start any one of these today and I encourage you to do so!

1. Donate what you no longer want or need. Help a good cause while clearing out the clutter that junks up your mind and your home. Donations can be given to charities. Smaller donations such as clothes, furniture or household items. Help those in need of housing by donating furniture, excess building supplies,

remodeling remnants, etc. Tired of your music, books, DVDs or video games? Trade them for free with other users via the web. Make a profit off of your used gear without the hassle of eBay listings. These donations and discounts can make a huge difference in the lives of those that are less fortunate, especially now. Plus, getting rid of the stuff that is taking up space will only gives you more room to breathe, think and relax.

2. Commit to a few months without TV, internet or cable. Your choice! Without the distraction of your weekly shows, you allow for more personal, family or friend time. Decide what is not necessary and do a trial run without it. If you can't stand the thought of going cold turkey, keep a log of how long you spend on the internet or watching TV at home per week. Those are the hours you could save yourself to do the things that you don't think you have time for.

3. Try to utilize all of your resources before re-using them. For instance, only do laundry when you absolutely need to or go through all of your plates or silverware before running the dishwasher. This will not only save you electricity, water and time but also make you aware of where you have excess.

4. Go through books, papers and old files. Shear what you don't need and donate the rest.

5. Eat more and dine out less. Save money and make family meals more important. Whatever happened to a home cooked family meal around the dinner table? Much less eating a meal sitting down and not on the go!

Reduce junk food as you grocery shop and fill up your fridge with organic fruits and veggies from the farmer's market (also saving yourself money!).

6. Make an ongoing priority list. Get "it" out of your mind and onto a tangible list. Use software like Microsoft Word to create a prioritized list of what you need to get at the grocery store, at target and even of the pesky 'to-dos' around the house. When you make a list on the computer, you have the ability to edit, move things up in priority and print it to take with you. This reduces the chances of a hundred post-it notes cluttering up your desk and home. Not to mention it

frees up your mind to focus on more important tasks than 'remember to get trash bags.'

7. Simplify your routine. Mornings should not be stressful "go" times. Take care of any of the 'to-dos' the night before. Have a simple self care routine that includes hygiene, nourishment and movement in the morning. Give yourself plenty of time to relax in your shower, prepare a healthy breakfast that gives you a boost of energy and do a few simple stretches. All of this can still happen in an hour to an hour and a half.

8. Know what you mean and say it! We expend a lot of energy holding grudges for situations that the other person has long forgotten, waiting for someone else to guess what we want and hoping things will just change on their own. Let's take a moment to remember that everyone thinks differently and very few of us can read minds. Our lives would all be a lot more fulfilling if we took the time to understand what we want in any given situation and then provided an explanation to those around us who could help foster the change.

9. Ask for help. Who says you have to do it all alone? If you're at work and feel behind, stuck or confused after trying to figure something out yourself, speak up! You'll take up less time stopping to ask for help than spinning your wheels for an hour trying to figure out what should be done. The same principle applies at home. Ask your spouse, a family member or a friend to give you a hand with a large project (or even the small ones!). Most of the time, they don't know you need help unless you ask.

10. Take a walk. Simplify your lifestyle with some good old fashioned fresh air. Take 15 minutes (or more!) to get outside either with your favorite person or just with your favorite thoughts about what you want in your life. This time is off limits for negative thoughts, anxiety, worry and stress. Only positive, future visualization of what you want your life to be like is appropriate to fill this time. Finding that your negative thoughts tiptoe in anyway? That's okay. Simply take a breath and imagine that worried scenario going exactly as you'd like it to and move on to the next positive thought.

Even if you choose one of these things to tackle, you'll be well on your way to a simpler lifestyle. Happy Simplifying.

CHAPTER SEVEN
DECLUTTER YOUR MIND BY DECLUTTERING YOUR HOUSE

It's been proven by many scientific and psychological studies past and present, that decluttering your house and living space, in turn, declutters your mind. Here are four different reasons minimizing your clutter benefits your brain:

1. Less to clean

If you consider all the different ornaments, trinkets and furniture that you spend time cleaning, they all add up to a huge amount of cleaning time that you wouldn't have to endure if those items were sold, given away or placed in self-storage. Most of us lead extremely busy lives and cleaning is a chore the majority of us would avoid if we could. Imagine how much time you would save cleaning if you downsized your clutter, leaving you much more energy and mental space to spend on other issues and activities.

2. Facing the real clutter

Although you'll have items that are sentimental and meaningful to you that you will want to keep, you will inevitably have a buildup of items that need to go. Working your way through all the items you love will force you to address the items you've been avoiding such as old paperwork, unwanted birthday and Christmas presents and other general clutter. You may find you've plenty of items that you don't feel ready to address through lack of time or facilities. This is even more reason to place them into cheap storage as your house is your headspace and moving them into a separate facility takes them out of your imminent surroundings and allows you to deal with them when you're ready.

3. Enjoying what you do have

Sometimes it can be really easy to collate items and knick-knacks, cramming them into your property without really displaying them or enjoying them. Items are only really worth anything if they can be accessed and enjoyed, no matter what their market value is. If you're finding that you don't have enough space to display your possessions properly and find you're struggling to display anything new, you'll be less able to enjoy what you do have because there's simply not enough room to place it where it can be enjoyed. Consider using a self-storage unit to halve the amount of items you have at home so the remainder can be enjoyed properly. Having a clean, well thought out home will give you a mental boost leaving you more able to relax in the place where you spend the most time.

4. Clutter equals stress

Having a cluttered home is stressful for many different reasons. Being unable to move around properly, clean properly and find the items you need exactly when you need them can be extremely frustrating and stressful. Often people's homes are a reflection of their mental state and hoarders, in particular, find that they are unable to let go of anything because of an emotional connection causing them to attach feelings and compulsive thoughts to all of their items. If you're struggling to let go, that doesn't make you a hoarder but it does reflect the fact that you might be unable to detach emotions from objects, which isn't a healthy path to go down.

Having a clear out involving car boots, charity donations and perhaps a self-storage unit means you'll feel you're more in control of your living situation and in turn your emotions. A stress-free space can be achieved by decluttering your home and there's nothing stopping you except a little time, effort and organization.

CONCLUSION

When you think of clutter, do you think of stuff or disorganization around your home? That is certainly one definition of clutter, but clutter is so much more than that. Clutter can be unfinished projects that are hanging over your head or tolerations that you put up with in life. Clutter is unhealthy relationships, bad habits, negative thoughts and destructive emotional states. Basically, clutter is anything that interferes with living your best life and being your best self.

Why care about the clutter? Clutter is an instant energy drain. Whether it's messy closets, a bad attitude, a job you don't like, or unpaid taxes, they all interfere with living a joyful and fulfilling life. When you get rid of the clutter, you love yourself enough to grow and be your best. You know the old saying, "Out with the old and in with the new". Addressing the clutter in your life opens the door for new and exciting things to happen. Every time I say goodbye to something that is no longer aligned with my best life, a new opportunity magically appears.

Lightning Source UK Ltd.
Milton Keynes UK
UKHW021909090220
358432UK00017B/363